D1272597

LEGO MANUFACTURERS

The Kristiansen Family

LEE SLATER

Checkerboard Library

An Imprint of Abdo Publishing
abdopublishing.com

3 1489 00686 6097

#2707

FREEPORT MEMORIAL LIBRARY

abdopublishing.com

Published by Abdo Publishing, a division of ABDO, PO Box 398166, Minneapolis, Minnesota 55439. Copyright © 2016 by Abdo Consulting Group, Inc. International copyrights reserved in all countries. No part of this book may be reproduced in any form without written permission from the publisher. Checkerboard Library™ is a trademark and logo of Abdo Publishing.

Printed in the United States of America, North Mankato, Minnesota
102015
012016

THIS BOOK CONTAINS
RECYCLED MATERIALS

Content Developer: Nancy Tuminelly
Design and Production: Mighty Media, Inc.
Series Editor: Paige Polinsky
Cover Photos: AP Images (center); Mighty Media (border)
Interior Photos: AP Images, p. 23; Corbis, pp. 9, 11, 15; Courtesy of The Strong®, Rochester, New York, p. 16; iStockphoto, p. 7; Shutterstock, pp. 5, 6, 13, 17, 18, 21, 24, 25, 27, 28, 29

Library of Congress Cataloging-in-Publication Data
Names: Slater, Lee, 1969- author.
Title: LEGO manufacturers : the Kristiansen family / by Lee Slater.
Description: Minneapolis, Minnesota : ABDO Publishing Company, [2016] |
    Series: Toy trailblazers | Includes index.
Identifiers: LCCN 2015030430 | ISBN 9781624039775
Subjects: LCSH: Kirk Christiansen, Ole, 1891-1958--Juvenile literature. |
    Kirk Christiansen, Godtfred, 1920-1995--Juvenile literature. | LEGO
    koncernen (Denmark)--History--Juvenile literature. | LEGO
    toys--History--Juvenile literature. | Toy
    industry--Denmark--History--Juvenile literature.
Classification: LCC TS2301.T7 S575 2016 | DDC 688.7/25--dc23
LC record available at http://lccn.loc.gov/2015030430

CONTENTS

Chapter 1

A FAMOUS
Toymaker Is Born

Ole Kirk Christiansen was born on April 7, 1891, in the village of Filskov, Denmark. He was the tenth child of Jens and Kirstine Christiansen. The Christiansens had little money. Jens worked on a nearby farm while Kirstine took care of the family. But these humble beginnings led to great success. Ole would grow up to create the LEGO empire.

Like most children in rural Denmark, Ole and his siblings worked very hard. They helped run the family farm. However, education was important to their parents. Jens and Kirstine wanted all of their children to learn to read and write. So at age six, Ole started going to school twice a week.

When not in school, Ole tended livestock. To pass the time, he carved small wooden figures. These wooden carvings were some of his only toys. Ole never expected he would become a famous toymaker!

Farming was one of Denmark's largest industries when Ole was growing up.

Chapter 2

Ole Builds
HIS LIFE

Ole's schooling ended when he was 14 years old. It was time for him to learn a trade. His older brother, Kristian, was a carpenter. Jens and Kirstine decided that Ole would become Kristian's **apprentice**. Ole worked alongside his brother for four years. In 1911, he was awarded a **journeyman**'s certificate.

In the early 1900s, many young men in Denmark learned carpentry. This led to too many workers and not enough jobs. Ole had to leave Denmark to find work. He worked as a carpenter in Germany for a year before moving to

Ole's carpentry training shaped his future. His woodworking skills made LEGO possible!

FUN FACT

Ole and Kirstine's new home in Billund was only about nine miles (14 km) from Ole's birthplace.

Norway. During the four years he lived in Norway, he met and married Kirstine Sorensen. In 1916, Ole and Kirstine settled in Billund, Denmark.

Ole used his savings to buy the Billund Carpentry Shop and Lumberyard. Ole's shop built homes, repaired items, and made furniture. Ole earned a reputation for quality work at an honest price. Meanwhile, he and Kirstine had started a family. Between 1917 and 1920, they had three sons. Their names were Johannes, Karl Georg, and Godtfred.

Chapter 3

LIFE Isn't Always Easy

Ole worked hard to provide for his family. But his business suffered during the **Great Depression**. The economy was bad, and jobs were scarce. People were building fewer homes and buying less furniture. As a result, Ole and his family almost went **bankrupt**.

But Ole saw that parents were willing to sacrifice some money to bring their children joy. So, he started building and selling **durable** wooden toys, and they sold well. He often accepted food as payment.

In 1932, tragedy struck. Kirstine died while giving birth to their fourth son, Gerhardt. Ole was left to raise the boys on his own. That same year, 12-year-old Godtfred became his father's main assistant. Together they made ironing boards, ladders, yo-yos, and wooden animals.

In 1934, Ole decided it was time to create his own **brand** name. He started with the Danish phrase *leg godt*. In English this means "play well." Ole combined the two words to create the name LEGO. The LEGO Group was officially born.

Ole's workshop was dedicated to quality work. Its carpenters were not afraid to get their hands dirty!

That same year, Ole married Sofie Jorgensen. And in 1935, they had a daughter, Ulla. Ole's life was starting to become less of a challenge.

Chapter 4

The First LEGO TOYS

By 1936, the company was producing more than 40 different toys. The workshop employed a small group of carpenters. Ole's personal motto was "Only the best is good enough." Godtfred carved this on a sign and hung it in the workshop.

Godtfred created many models for new toys. He and Ole drew patterns for the other carpenters to follow. The LEGO toys were expensive, but they were built to last. **Consumers** were happy to pay a bit more for such high quality.

In 1942, the LEGO Group factory and warehouse burned down. All the plans, materials, tools, models, and products were lost. Before Ole began rebuilding, he thought about the company's future.

FUN FACT

One of the most popular original LEGO toys was a wooden duck on wheels.

The LEGO carpenters worked hard in the business of play.

Homes and household products were not in high demand. But everyone loved LEGO toys. Ole wanted to focus on these popular items. He decided that the new LEGO Group would only make toys.

Chapter 5

PLASTIC
Classics

All of the original LEGO toys were carved from wood. But in the mid-1940s, plastic became a new material for toy makers. **Consumers** were eager to buy colorful plastic toys. In 1947, the Christiansen family purchased an expensive injection molding machine. This new machine allowed them to **mass-produce** plastic toys.

At first, Ole's workers thought it was a strange idea. Then Ole showed them some plastic building blocks manufactured by a British toy company. The blocks could be put together and pulled apart. Ole asked his designers to create a mold for a similar toy. In 1949, LEGO began manufacturing plastic building blocks. LEGO's Automatic Binding Bricks were the earliest versions of the LEGO bricks we know today.

FUN FACT

Today's LEGO molds are very **accurate**. There are only 18 flawed pieces out of every million produced!

All of Ole's sons eventually joined the family business. Godtfred was the managing director of the company. Karl was the director of plastic product manufacturing. Gerhardt was the director of wood product manufacturing. And Johannes was responsible for shipping and distribution.

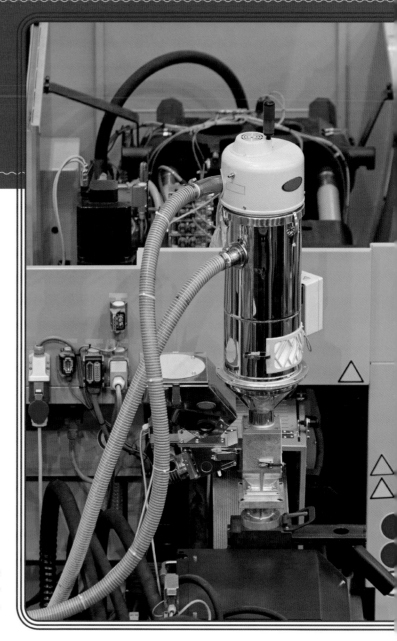

Toy companies still use injection molding machines to manufacture plastic toys.

Chapter 6

Life of A LEGO BRICK

LEGO no longer makes its products in a small workshop. Today's LEGO bricks are manufactured around the world! There are LEGO Group factories in many countries including Denmark, Mexico, and the United States. The production of LEGO bricks is almost completely **automated**.

First, trucks filled with colored plastic **granules** arrive at the factory. Giant hoses suck up the granules and dump them into huge metal **silos**. Pipes transport the granules to the injection molding machines.

The molding machine heats the granules to 450 degrees Fahrenheit (232°C). The machine feeds the melted plastic into molds. These are metal containers with compartments shaped like hollow LEGO bricks. The machine uses pressure to **accurately** shape the bricks. The bricks cool for about 10 seconds and are then **ejected**.

A conveyor belt drops the finished LEGO bricks into boxes. A robotic truck moves full boxes to the decoration area. Here, a printing machine stamps details onto the bricks. The next step is collecting the right

The LEGO factories have produced more than 400 billion bricks since 1958.

pieces to make complete LEGO packages. Boxes roll on conveyor belts underneath bins that hold different colored LEGO bricks. The bins release a set number of pieces into each box.

Finally, humans take over to finish the job. Workers fold the boxes and add instructions to each one. They check each box to make sure there are no mistakes.

Chapter 7

A NEW NAME
and a New System

In 1953, LEGO Automatic Binding Bricks were renamed *LEGO Mursten*, or "LEGO Bricks." The next year, Godtfred attended a toy fair in England. One buyer said that most toys didn't have any system. The buyer wanted a group of similar toys that could be used together. Godtfred liked this idea. And the **interlocking** LEGO bricks were the perfect product to use!

In 1955, LEGO launched its System of Play. The first product was called Town Plan No. 1. The base had printed markings for streets and crosswalks. There were plastic people, trees, road signs, and cars. The instructions encouraged kids to create their own original towns!

But the LEGO bricks didn't always stick together well.

FUN FACT

There are more than 915 million ways to combine six eight-stud LEGO bricks.

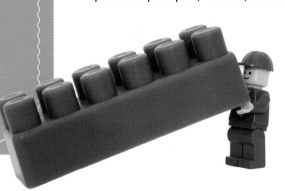

LEGO's System of Play
allowed children to think outside the box!

So Godtfred designed a better brick. It had three tubes instead of a
hollow space. This new design was called a stud-and-tube locking system.
The successful new LEGO brick was **patented** on January 28, 1958.

Chapter 8

The Family BUSINESS

Ole Kirk Christiansen died on March 11, 1958. Godtfred became the company's new president. By then, LEGO products were being sold throughout Europe. But Godtfred was ready to expand. He started exporting LEGO toys to Canada, Asia, Australia, Africa, and the United States.

Godtfred's leadership and the LEGO System of Play boosted the **brand**'s success. LEGO products became extremely successful around the world. In 1967, more than 18 million LEGO sets were sold worldwide!

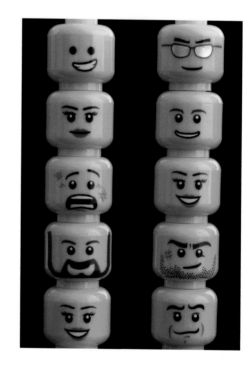

The original LEGO minifigures did not have faces. Today there are more than 600 different expressions available.

FUN FACT

A mistake on Kjeld's birth certificate spelled his last name with a K. The Christiansen descendants have spelled their name "Kristiansen" ever since.

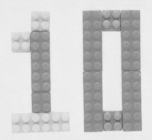

CHARACTERISTICS

In 1963, Godtfred presented the company with ten product **characteristics**. He wanted every toy produced by the LEGO Group to offer these things.

1. Unlimited play **potential**
2. For girls and for boys
3. Fun for every age
4. Year-round play
5. Healthy, quiet play
6. Long hours of play
7. Development, imagination, creativity
8. The more LEGO, the greater the value
9. Extra sets available
10. Quality in every detail

During the 1970s, the first LEGO **minifigures** were introduced. And in 1977, LEGO launched its Expert Builder series. These models used motors and gears to move. Themed sets, such as the LEGO Castle and LEGO Space sets, were another first.

Each generation of the family increased the company's success. The legacy continued when Godtfred's son, Kjeld Kirk Kristiansen, became company president in 1979.

Chapter 9

A True GAME CHANGER

K jeld led the company in many new directions. He founded the annual LEGO Prize in 1985. This international award recognized efforts to help children. The company also sponsored international LEGO building competitions. The first LEGO World Cup was held in 1988.

Under Kjeld's leadership, LEGO products started using new technology. LEGO sets began including electric lights, motors, and sounds. The company released more and more products each year. The LEGO Group also opened LEGOLAND theme parks, clothing stores, and a hotel.

During this expansion, video games increased in popularity. Many kids became more interested in computers than building blocks. LEGO competed with some computer games of its own. But the world of play was changing fast. By 2004, The LEGO Group was losing money. If the business didn't do something, it would go **bankrupt**.

Kjeld realized it was time for a **drastic** change. He stepped down as president and hired Jorgen Vig Knudstorp to lead the company.

Knudstorp was an expert at saving failing businesses. For the first time in
LEGO history, someone outside the family was leading the way.

Chapter 10

Rebuilding the
LEGO BRAND

The Kristiansen family still owned the LEGO Group. But it was Knudstorp's job to turn the company around. To do this, he had to manage cash flow.

Cash flow refers to the movement of money through a company. Money entering a company is called income. Money leaving a company is called expense. If more money leaves than comes in, the company fails to make a profit. A successful company takes in more money than it spends.

Knudstorp **analyzed** the cost of making each LEGO product. He eliminated products that cost too much or didn't sell well. For example, the LEGO computer games weren't very popular. And it would cost too much to improve these games. Ole's vision was about quality, not quantity.

FUN FACT

The LEGO bricks sold in 2012 could circle the world more than 18 times.

Knudstorp wanted LEGO "to compete not by being the biggest but by being the best."

But what would inspire kids to choose LEGOs over computer screens? Knudstorp invested a lot of the company's money in research. The LEGO Group needed to understand how modern kids played. That's where the Future Lab came in!

Chapter 11

The FUTURE LAB

T he Future Lab is a group of about 50 LEGO researchers, **engineers**, and designers. Its job is to invent new play experiences for children everywhere. Knudstorp says, "It's about discovering what's obviously LEGO, but has never been seen before."

Future Lab researchers partner with universities and independent researchers. Together, they study current best-selling toys. They play with kids and talk to them about their likes and dislikes.

Meanwhile, Future Lab designers research popular movies and computer games. They follow trendy fashions, magazines, and websites. They are always looking for inspirational ideas.

The Future Lab holds a special meeting every year. Associates spend a week on the Mediterranean coast of Spain. The

FUN FACT

In 2014, *The LEGO Movie* was the highest grossing film in the United Kingdom. It was fifth highest in the United States.

The Future Lab is improving LEGO brick by brick.
It builds on the ideas of kids and engineers alike!

Future Lab employees bring research, samples, and plenty of imagination.
They **brainstorm**, sketch, and design future products. The work is hard,
but it's all about play!

Chapter 12

The Kristiansen FAMILY TODAY

Ole's descendants are currently among the wealthiest people in Denmark. The family has come a long way from its humble farm beginnings. Ole's strong **work ethic** has guided the Kristiansens to great success.

The LEGO Group is owned by KIRKBI A/S and the LEGO Foundation. KIRKBI A/S is the investment company of the Kristiansen family. Some of its investments are in **renewable energy**. The LEGO Group hopes to fully rely on renewable energy by 2020. The LEGO Foundation is a charity. It uses play to improve education for children worldwide.

The Kristiansen family is **dedicated** to making a positive difference in the world. LEGO toys continue to inspire and delight children all over the world. And as Ole always said, "Only the best is good enough."

FUN FACT

LEGO has been the Kristiansen family business for more than 75 years.

The LEGO Group recycles 90 percent of its production waste.

TIMELINE

1891
Ole Kirk Christiansen is born in Filskov, Denmark, on April 7.

1932
Ole's wife, Kirstine, dies.

1942
The factory burns down. A new factory is built for the purpose of manufacturing toys only.

1916
Ole opens his own business making wooden household items.

1934
Ole marries Sofie Jorgensen. The LEGO name is born.

1949
The first Automatic Binding Bricks are produced.

FUN FACT

In 2000, LEGO was named "Toy of the Century" by *Fortune* magazine and the Toy Retailers Association.

1953

Automatic Binding Bricks are renamed LEGO Bricks.

1979

Kjeld Kirk Kristiansen, Ole's grandson, becomes president of the company.

1958

Ole dies of a heart attack. Godtfred Kirk Christiansen becomes head of the company.

2004

The first non-family member, Jorgen Vig Knudstorp, becomes president of the company.

Glossary

accurate – free of errors.

analyze – to determine the meaning of something by breaking down its parts.

apprentice – a person who learns a trade or a craft from a skilled worker.

automate – to use machines rather than people to do jobs, especially in factories.

bankrupt – legally declared unable to pay something owed.

brainstorm – when people get together to come up with ideas or a solution to a problem.

brand – a category of products made by a particular company and all having the same company name.

characteristic – a quality or a feature of something.

consumer – a person who buys and uses products and services.

dedicate – to give a lot of time and energy to something.

drastic – serious and likely to have important or long-lasting effects.

durable – able to exist for a long time without weakening.

eject – to remove from inside something.

engineer – someone who is specially trained to design and build machines or large structures such as bridges and roads.

To learn more about Toy Trailblazers, visit booklinks.abdopublishing.com. These links are routinely monitored and updated to provide the most current information available.

granule – a small, firm particle of a substance.

Great Depression – the period from 1929 to 1942 of worldwide economic trouble. There was little buying or selling, and many people could not find work.

interlock – to join or hook together.

journeyman – a trained worker who has completed an apprenticeship.

mass-produce – to use machines to make large amounts of identical things in a factory.

minifigure – a small, plastic figurine manufactured by the LEGO Group.

patent – to apply for and receive the exclusive right to make or sell an invention. This right lasts for a certain period of time.

potential – what a person is capable of achieving in the future.

renewable energy – power from sources that can never be used up, such as wind, tides, sunlight, and geothermal heat.

silo – a tall, round tower used to store items.

work ethic – the principle that hard work is valuable and worthy of reward.